Where Does It Go?

Where Does Mail Go?

by Charlie W. Sterling

Bullfrog
Books

Ideas for Parents and Teachers

Bullfrog Books let children practice reading informational text at the earliest reading levels. Repetition, familiar words, and photo labels support early readers.

Before Reading

- Discuss the cover photo. What does it tell them?

- Look at the picture glossary together. Read and discuss the words.

Read the Book

- "Walk" through the book and look at the photos. Let the child ask questions. Point out the photo labels.

- Read the book to the child, or have him or her read independently.

After Reading

- Prompt the child to think more. Ask: Have you ever mailed a letter? Did you wonder where it went after you mailed it?

Bullfrog Books are published by Jump!
5357 Penn Avenue South
Minneapolis, MN 55419
www.jumplibrary.com

Library of Congress Cataloging-in-Publication Data

Names: Sterling, Charlie W., author.
Title: Where does mail go? / by Charlie W. Sterling.
Description: Minneapolis: Jump!, Inc., [2021]
Series: Where does it go? | Includes index.
Audience: Ages 5–8. | Audience: Grades K–1.
Identifiers: LCCN 2020002953 (print)
LCCN 2020002954 (ebook)
ISBN 9781645275503 (library binding)
ISBN 9781645275510 (paperback)
ISBN 9781645275527 (ebook)
Subjects: LCSH: Postal service—Juvenile literature.
Classification: LCC HE6078 .S74 2021 (print)
LCC HE6078 (ebook) | DDC 383—dc23
LC record available at https://lccn.loc.gov/2020002953
LC ebook record available at https://lccn.loc.gov/2020002954

Editor: Jenna Gleisner
Designer: Molly Ballanger

Photo Credits: Mega Pixel/Shutterstock, cover; James Crawford/Dreamstime, 1; Monkey Business Images/Shutterstock, 3; udovichenko/Shutterstock, 4 (foreground), 22tr, 23br; Zocha_K/iStock, 4 (background), 22tr; DougSchneiderPhoto/iStock, 5; Georgesheldon/Dreamstime, 6–7, 22tl; David R. Frazier Photolibrary, Inc./Alamy, 8–9, 23tr; Joanna Dorota/Shutterstock, 9; Greg K__ca/Shutterstock, 10; Philip Pilosian/Shutterstock, 11; UPI/Alamy, 12–13, 22br; Trong Nguyen/Shutterstock, 14–15, 22bm, 23bl; Jim West/Alamy, 16–17, 22bl, 23tl; Loveischiangrai/Shutterstock, 18 (foreground); Imagenet/Shutterstock, 18 (background); Syda Productions/Dreamstime, 19, 20–21; DNY59/iStock, 24.

Printed in the United States of America at Corporate Graphics in North Mankato, Minnesota.

Table of Contents

In the Mail

Meg Alaniz
2274 Main Street
Seattle, WA 98109

Dana Nelson
2401 Valley Drive
Philadelphia, PA 19108

Meg writes Dana a letter.

She puts it in the mailbox.
Then what happens to it?

A carrier picks it up.
Why?
She will drive
it to a plant.

mail
truck

mail
carrier

UNITED STATES
POSTAL SERVICE

UNITED STATES
POSTAL SERVICE

plant

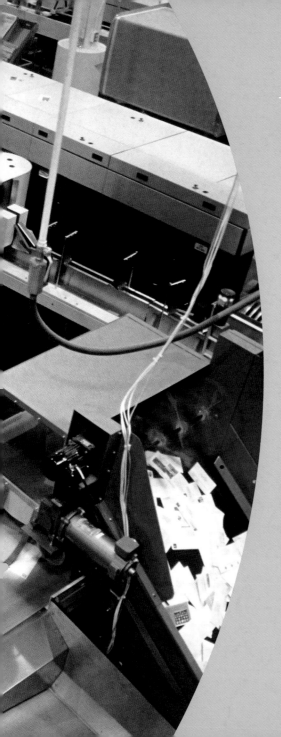

A camera reads
the ZIP code.

Neat!

Letters are sorted
by their code.

Dana Nelson
2401 Valley Drive
Philadelphia, PA 19108

ZIP code

9

Some letters go by truck.

Others go on airplanes!

These letters are going far.

Cool!

The letters go to
another plant.

They are sorted again.

Where does Meg's letter go?

To Dana's post office.

A carrier delivers it.
Where?

17

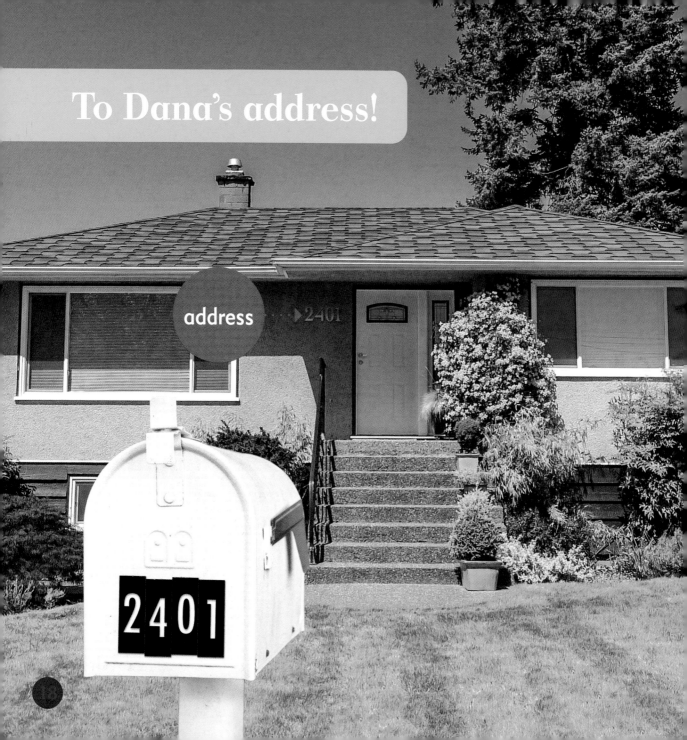

To Dana's address!

address

2401

2401

Thank you!

Dana gets the letter!

She writes back.

Cool!

Where Mail Goes

What happens to mail after it leaves your home? Take a look!

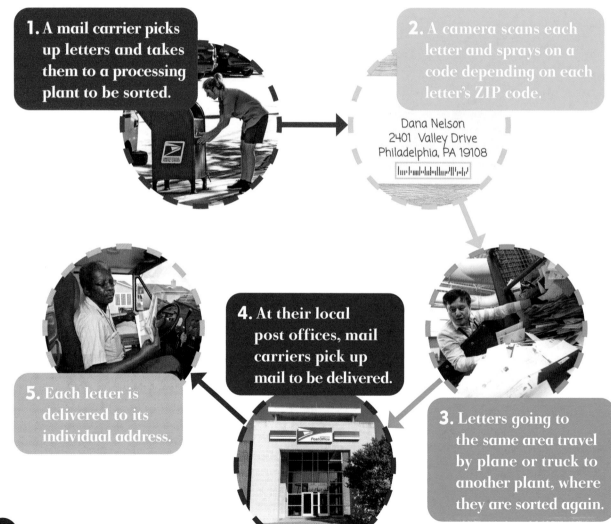

1. A mail carrier picks up letters and takes them to a processing plant to be sorted.

2. A camera scans each letter and sprays on a code depending on each letter's ZIP code.

Dana Nelson
2401 Valley Drive
Philadelphia, PA 19108

4. At their local post offices, mail carriers pick up mail to be delivered.

5. Each letter is delivered to its individual address.

3. Letters going to the same area travel by plane or truck to another plant, where they are sorted again.

Picture Glossary

delivers
Takes something to someone.

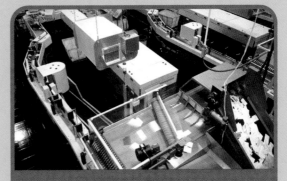

plant
A building and the equipment inside that carry out a process.

post office
The place where people go to buy stamps and to send letters and packages.

Dana Nelson
2401 Valley Drive
Philadelphia, PA 19108

ZIP code
A number given to each delivery area in the United States to speed up the sorting and delivery of mail.

Index

Parker Smith
451 Lakewood St.
Easley, SC 29640

Andrew Lee
421 Parker Street
Westwood, NJ 07675

To Learn More

FACT SURFER

Finding more information is as easy as 1, 2, 3.

❶ Go to www.factsurfer.com

❷ Enter "wheredoesmailgo" into the search box.

❸ Choose your book to see a list of websites.